Bella Cortez

CRAFTY CORTEZ SISTERS
The Story

I wrote this book to share the story about my business, how we got started, and hope this first book helps me become a better writer in the future. At first, I didn't think I could write my own book, but April (my bonus-mom) told me I could do it and she would help me... so, here it is. I hope you enjoy my story. ~ Bella Cortez

Author	Bella Julianna Cortez
Editor	April Mae Monterrosa
Publisher	Live from the Southside

Copyright © 2020 by Live from the Southside

All rights reserved. No part of this publication may be reproduced, distributed, or transmitted in any form or by any means, including photocopying, recording, or other electronic or mechanical methods, without the prior written permission of the publisher. For permission requests, write to the publisher at LiveFromTheSouthside@Gmail.com

The Crafty Cortez Sisters: The Story

Table of Contents

Chapter 1 How it started 1

Chapter 2 When we got home 4

Chapter 3 New school year arrives 6

Chapter 4 Market day 8

Chapter 5 Working on more crafts 11

Chapter 6 Working on staycation 14

Chapter 7 More crafts! 18

Chapter 8 Our 3rd one 21

Chapter 9 My future goals 24

Chapter 1: How it all started

   While on a family trip to Port Aransas, Texas, my sister Ruby and I were taking a walk on the beach with April (our bonus mom and her mom Norma or as we call her, "Mrs.G".) I mentioned how I wanted to earn my own money to buy more clothes and accessories for my dolls. I love to play with American Girl Dolls and I know their accessories are expensive. I told April that when we get older I'd like for my sister Ruby and I to start our own business. April said that it was a great idea and that if we wanted to start our own business now, she would help us. My sister and I got excited and happy that we were going to start our own business, make our own money, and couldn't wait to get back home to begin.

Our bonus-mom (April) suggested we get a binder or a notebook to write ideas for our business name and what we want to create to sell. She also told us she would help us with marketing since that's what she does for a living. We continued our walk on the beach and thought of names for our business; it was harder than I thought it would be to come up with the perfect name. So many things went through my mind and kept on wondering what it was going to feel like when we had our own customers. I was so excited, I wanted to go to the nearest store to buy a notebook and start writing down all my ideas. Instead, I relaxed and enjoyed the rest of our trip.

Chapter 2: When we got home

After our beach trip, I was super excited to go home to tell my oldest sister Destiny about starting our own business since she didn't go on the trip. As soon as I was done unpacking, I put a lot of paper in my binder and started writing down all my ideas. By then, my oldest sister Destiny had gotten home and I was able to share my good news with her. I wrote down quite a few different names and couldn't decide which one to pick. When I shared my ideas with my Dad, April, and my sisters Ruby and Destiny, we all liked the name, "Crafty Cortez Sisters", including me.

After our bonus-mom helped us create our logo, the ideas just kept pouring in and we decided to decorate picture frames as our first business idea. We went to Hobby Lobby the next day (and stopped at Starbucks first as we always do when we go on our "3 musketeer adventures.) to stock up on supplies to start creating our merchandise.

As soon as April shared our business on her social media, we instantly received tons of support from her friends; some even donated money to help us with supply costs. As soon as we got back to April's house we got to work. We had the music blasting with the playlist we created on Spotify, having are usual girl talk, and painting our frames; it was a lot of fun. The day after that we added gems and decorations to the frames. I didn't think all this was going to be so much fun, but it was.

During that week, April posted our finished frames on her social media and they were sold out in 2 days. We couldn't believe it and were very grateful to everyone that bought our frames. People started to put orders in for our frames and while we were creating those we also started on decorating headbands. These weren't as easy to make but using our mannequins helped out a lot.

Bella's Ideas

1. Bella's and Roby's crafts
2. Crafty Sisters
3. Crafting
4. Cats and pandas

Brands	Color
1. B&R crafts	1. ▆▆ purple and blue
2. CS	2. ▆▆ Pink
3. Crafting	3. ▆▆ red
4. Cats and pandas	4. ▢ Black and white

Chapter 3: New school year arrives

Schedules changed a bit when our bonus-mom launched her magazine and that meant we weren't going to be at her house as much as we usually were and where we normally work on our crafts at. So, the Crafty Cortez Sisters workshop moved to our house and where we finished the second batch of our crafts.

Our sister Jasmine decided she wanted to start making her own jewelry to make her own money too and we all started working together at the table at our house everyday. When school was about to start, we took a break from all business stuff to focus on getting ready for the new school year and while we waited for our next shipment of supplies to come in.

Things started to happen so fast! We had our first interview with Live from the Southside Magazine and sold our crafts at our first market on the Southside of San Antonio. It was really exciting how all these things we never experienced were happening. As soon as our supplies came in we got to work. Even going to school didn't stop me; every break I had, I worked on our crafts and accessories till they got finished. All four of my sisters helped out too.

We had a big batch of crafts to sell on our first market day. April told us there was going to be food trucks and other craft vendors we could meet and learn from. Even though I was excited, I was really tired because I stayed up late working on my crafts so that I could finish as much as I could.

CRAFTY CORTEZ SISTERS

BY BELLA & RUBY

Bella & Ruby Cortez

The Crafty Cortez Sisters are young entrepreneurs from South San Antonio, Texas that have a love for crafting and accessories.

You can check out their merch on Facebook & Instagram!

@CraftyCortezSisters

Chapter 4: Market day

Market day was finally here! We packed everything the night before and woke up early so we could gather all of our things to be ready and leave on time. My sister Ruby and I wore matching outfits and t-shirts with our logo on them that April's friend had made and gifted to us. After a Starbucks stop, we arrived at the market and my dad and sisters were already there setting up our table and canopy.

My sisters and I took all of our crafts out of the boxes and set them up nicely on our table. Ruby and I set up our merch on one side and our sister Jasmine set hers up on the other. At first, Jasmine and I thought that no one was going to buy anything from us and we'd be the only vendors that didn't sell anything. But, we were wrong. About 30 minutes into the market, we had our first customers. We couldn't believe it was happening; our hard work was paying off and we started making our own money.

Some of our families came out to the market to support us, bought some of our stuff, and a few of them even let us keep the change. Ms. Cindy, a friend of April's, bought most of our picture frames; we were especially grateful to her for supporting our new little business. We sold most of our stuff even though it wasn't busy the whole day. I was the one in charge of keeping track of the money and it was exciting as I saw more and more come in.

We did take a break to look around and check out some of the other vendors; Rudy bought something but I didn't. The market was a bit different than what I expected but, all the vendors had to be spaced out because of Covid-19.

When we finished the market, we packed up all our things and headed home. When we put all our stuff up, we sorted all the money we made and paid my Dad out for the money he loaned us for supplies. The few frames we had left, April helped us out by selling them to her friends on her social media.

Chapter 5: Working on more crafts

Our second market was a few weeks away and what really made me look forward to that one was that it was going to be at Coffeecionado; my favorite coffee house.

We decided to make necklaces and more picture frames to sell. Ruby and I had been at April's house for a few days and when we found out our supplies came in, we were ready to get to work. We decided to change it up a bit and used stencils and charms. I asked my sister Jasmine if I could try making the necklaces she was because I really wanted to learn. They were a lot easier to make than I thought.

The weekend of the market, April planned a girl's staycation for us. Before we left, we were able to see our Aunt Melissa and tell her all about our business and the markets. She ended up buying a few of the necklaces Jasmine made for her daughter, our cousin Janessa.

That Thursday night, we finished up all our crafts, packed them up, and went back to April's house so when we were done with school, we'd make our way downtown to the hotel we were staying in for the weekend. Our first night of our staycation was super fun. We had dinner on the Riverwalk at the Hard Rock Café, walked around downtown, ate gelato on Houston Street, and relaxed before bedtime at the hotel. We had a cool city view of the Tower of Americas right outside our hotel roon window.

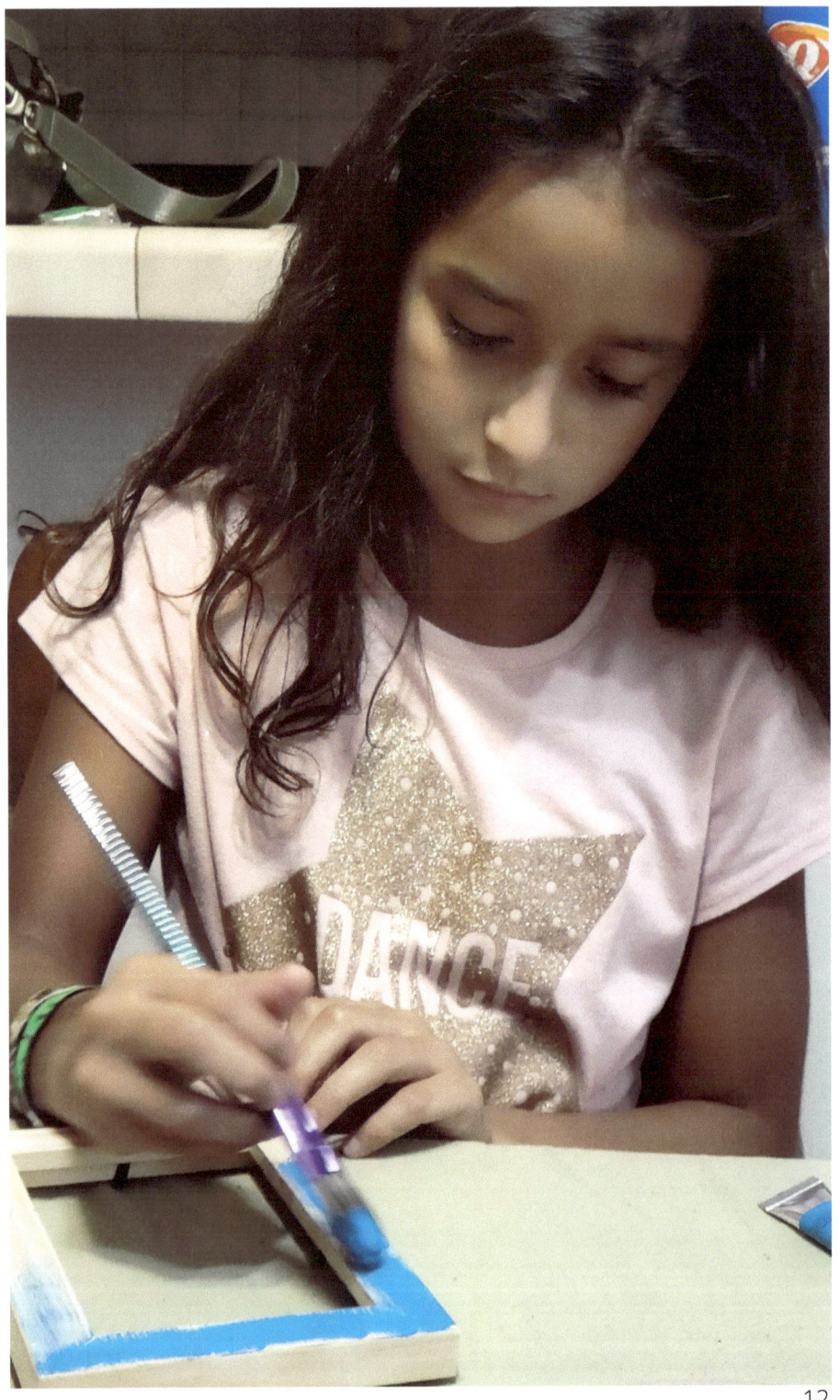

Chapter 6: Working on staycation

    Morning came fast and even though we woke up really early and I was tired, we got to see the sunrise over the city. After a nice warm shower, I was fully awake, got dressed up, and danced in front of the big mirror in our room while my hair air dried. Ruby and I were dressed and ready to go and waiting for April to finish getting ready and put on her lipstick. (We laughed and asked her why she even bothers putting any on since it gets all over her mask.)

I wanted to make a quick stop at Starbucks, but since we were going to a coffee house, I decided to get some from there, plus we had to wait for our Uber to pick us up. There was a long day ahead of us, so we made sure to eat our tacos that our Dad brought for us and the apple that the hotel manager gave us.

It was time to set up for our market day and as usual, I was excited. My sister Jasmine was supposed to be with us that day but didn't feel good and stayed home. Our crafts were not selling fast. Instead, Ruby and I walked around to see the other vendors and met Chamoy y Mas, a chamoy and candy business. I was so happy! I love chamoy and bought a chamoy covered candy apple.

After walking around the market, we went back to our table and my sister Jasmine's jewelry and some of our frames started selling too. When the market was over, we packed up and took another walk around the market one last time. The chamoy business gave April a sample of each of their candies for us to try. I wanted them all. When we left the market, we were all really tired. We did make money though.

Chapter 7: More crafts!

My Dad gave April, Ruby, and I a ride back to the hotel from the coffee house. We rested and relaxed for a bit at the hotel after our long day at the market. One of April's high school friends showed up at the hotel to meet us and give us a big box of things. There were nail polishes, makeup, Hello Kitty things, and some really cool sequin tennis shoes. After our staycation was over, we went back to April's house.

April told us that another friend of hers had dropped off a box of surprises at her house. Ruby and I were so excited to get there to see what it was. When we got to her house, the first thing we did was open the box up. It was a huge box of craft supplies! There were so many neat things inside that gave me lots of new crafting ideas.

The next day we had to wake up really early to go to our house to get ready to go to school. Still, we were thinking of ideas on what to make with all the craft supplies that were given to us.

After I got home from school, I was ready to work on things. My sisters Raven and Jasmine cooked dinner but I was still hungry. I called April and asked her if she could bring us McDonald's, and she did. When she brought our food to our house, she had another box of craft supplies that a different friend gave her for us. A lot of it was Christmas themed which we were glad to have since the holidays were right around the corner. We showed my sister Jasmine and she had a lot of great ideas too.

After we ate dinner, I asked my Dad if I could work on some of my crafts and he said it was ok. We had another market coming up and I wanted to make sure we had our crafts ready to sell. The room we were crafting in was a mess and we had to clean it up and organize things since we had new craft supplies and new crafts we made.

Chapter 8: Our 3rd one

Another early morning to get ready for market day. Can you believe we are now at our third one? After we showered and got dressed, April helped do our hair. Ruby and I wore a side ponytail and April put flowers in them.

We were running on schedule and even had extra time for April to take us to Starbucks. (My favorite is the Vanilla Bean Frap with extra, extra caramel.) While we were at Starbucks my Dad and sisters Raven and Jasmine were at the Whataburger across the street getting us breakfast.

It was a cool morning. April was driving with the windows down and the sunroof open and even though we were cold, we like to be on the road with the windows down. On our way to the market, we saw a big painting of Selena on the wall of a convenient store. My sister Ruby is a big Selena fan and wanted to take a picture in front of it. Me, I stayed in the car where it was warm. As usual, before any market, we take pictures and video to share all the information with our social media pages about the market we are selling at. Sometimes it takes a few times to get it right but we manage to do so.

People came to the market early, including some of our family. They bought some of Jasmine's necklaces, my frames, and other accessories we made. By the time the afternoon came, the weather warmed up; then, it got really hot. Luckily there was a food truck with different kinds of snacks, including funnel cake, and mangonadas. I ordered a mangonada and it was so good, I finished it all. April ordered us McDonald's on UberEats and they delivered it to us at the market. I was still full from the mangonada but, I love me some McDonald's.

We sold some of our things and my cousin Janessa and her mom, my Aunt Melissa stopped by the market to pick up the bracelets they had ordered from my sister Jasmine. I noticed my sister Jasmine made an ocean themed bracelet and I bought it from her. (I love ocean and mermaid themed things.) That market day was really hot but we did sell some of our crafts and accessories and made money.

Chapter 9: My future goals

We have now sold our crafts and accessories at 5 markets, an event for the Magik Theatre, and at the Scooby Doo Van of San Antonio Southside Chapter Launch. I am also the first kid writer for Live from the Southside Magazine. I plan to keep working at my craft and accessories business and hope to gain more experience as a young entrepreneur and business owner.

My goal and plan for the future is to own a boutique and have employees run it for me while I attend college to become a pediatrician. One of the biggest lessons I have learned so far is that you have to take your business seriously if you want to make money. You can't spend all the money you make right away because you have to use some of it to buy the supplies you need to continue making your crafts and accessories.

One day I would like to help other kids start their own businesses too. If they need help with getting the word out to other people. I can always ask my bonus-mom April to meet with them along with their parents to offer advice on how to start and what steps to take to start a business. (She handles all our marketing, advertising, and public relations.)

I like to think about how my life is gonna be and what the future is going to be like as a Crafty Cortez Sister. I often wonder things like: is my business going to grow? Will I have more customers? Will we keep doing this as a business? And what will we do next in our business? I don't have all the answers to these questions just yet but, one thing for sure... I don't want to stop. ~ Bella

Follow on Social Media:

Author - Bella Julianna Cortez
Facebook & Instagram: @CraftyCortezSisters

Editor - April Mae Monterrosa
Facebook, Instagram, & Twitter: @AprilMaeMedia

Publisher - Live from the Southside
Facebook, Instagram, & Twitter: @SouthsideSATX
southsidesanantonio.com

www.ingramcontent.com/pod-product-compliance
Lightning Source LLC
Chambersburg PA
CBHW041944240526
45473CB00033B/509